AN ETHIC

AN ETHIC

POEMS BY CHRISTINA DAVIS

NIGHTBOAT BOOKS
CALLICOON, NEW YORK

for my mother Beverly J. Davis

and in loving memory

of my father John H. Davis (1938-2006)

The poem is an ethic.

JEAN COCTEAU

An ethic   ethic: ethos …
what other words
can be found? Awe, perhaps—

GEORGE OPPEN

FOREWORD

Do we call it "loss" when the familiar is scalpeled away, even if the process makes visible the ligatures that bind us to others?

Do we call abandonment "loneliness" even if we recognize that "Into the entirety/ one is invited"?

How do we name those long, naked moments *before* the possibility of transformation?

The poems of *An Ethic* are gnomic. Christina Davis hones a spare lyric line ruptured by silence and space.

Oppen's *Of Being Numerous* haunts the collection. But *An Ethic* emerges from a space more intimate and familial than Oppen's.

Like snail horns and as sensitive, the poems tap their way into a mere parenthesis of our shared condition, they make contact and withdraw. But from the clarity of that almost unbearable intimacy, they project the hugeness of difference, solitude, recognition.

An Ethic is a book marked by severely understated wordplay, irruptive emphases and implications stropped on hardbitten lineation. The precise, restrained, constantly self-adjusting grammar enacts a form of discretion, a code of relation to language and world, a humility. Her poetic line is like a thin railing along the edge of a fathomless vertigo.

In their brevities, the poems are conscious of their own impoverishment, their limitations. The large white space of the page nearly swallows the modest phalanxes of words and overhowls them. Not quite.

Imagine poems as vitreous floaters crossing an eye focused on oblivion.

Imbricated with myth, but not grandeur.

An Ethic. Here is a book that has flapped up out of the startled dark of a parent's death. Into the moment of recognition of a life apart. A part of life.

The syntax, precise and probing, repeatedly extends beyond only apparent completions, beyond easy finalities, into an always unforeseen. As though a living hand were reaching out of the poem and—

FORREST GANDER

ACKNOWLEDGMENTS

Grateful acknowledgment is made to the publications in which these poems (or their earlier incarnations) first appeared: *Futurepoem Blog*, *The Occupy Wall Street Poetry Anthology*; *Pleiades*; *Plume*, *Revolutionesque*; *Tuesday: An Art Journal*, *Zoland Poetry* and *The Sonnets: Translating & Rewriting Shakespeare*. I would also like to thank Forrest Gander, Stephen Motika and the inimitable staff of Nightboat Books for accompanying this book into being. Additional thanks to my colleagues at Harvard University and to the MacDowell Colony and the Merrill House for providing me with a space (and a community with whom) to ponder the questions at the core of this book.

An Ethic would not have come into existence without the wisdom and beneficence of the following individuals it has been my privilege to exist among: my brother and nephew Robert and Ryan Davis, my cousin Leigh Hays, and my aunt Tona Barkley; our family friends Jim Butler and Carol & Jim Dooling; and my dear companions, friends and mentors—Miranda Field, Jorie Graham, Odile & Britten Harter, Jane Hirshfield, Dorothea Lasky, Richard McCollum, Susan Mitchell, Kathleen Ossip, Linda Siptroth Porter, Chloe Garcia Roberts, Tom Sleigh, Christopher Tambos, Zack & Marla Vogel, Catherine Watson, Jeffrey Yang, and the staff of Three Lives Books in Greenwich Village. And to Linda Oppen and her own beloved father to whose dark and blazing truths these poems are apprenticed.

And for my parents, whose lives were and are an ethic.

PART ONE

AN ETHIC

There is no this or that world.

One is not more or less
admitted. Into the entirety

one is invited
and to the entirety
one comes.

There is no this or that world,

only the long illusion we are landlord,
the never-ending study
of anotherness, the ark of ilks and kinds.

It is a later wilderness

in which we find ourselves,
it is an Our thought
if we but find our selves,

we will find that we dwell on the one earth.

I hope we are found
to have lived

on no this or that earth.

ALL THE ARCHITECTURES

And then he closed the mouth, from which we had meant,
and the body, which had taken such time to be established,
and then we each something different saw let go
the man from his kind, living being a kind of violence

of direction. And with him

went all

    that was

wall in us.

FURTHERMORE

It was something to let him go.

It was a having to believe, furthermore,

in the voyage
of the other, a Ulysses

without an Ithaca,

was to speak
of the sea
without speech
of the shore—

and to have for a body

the going away of the body, to have for eyes
the going away of the eyes. And for hearing,

a silence, where once
were people.

And for comfort, a dwelling
before each
steps into that weather
of which all
strangers speak.

INSTEAD OF A HEADSTONE

And then we turned to our mother
who was life.

         It felt a defection
from our father,

but on his gone behalf she led us
from his deathbed

         and returned us

to the living, whose wars were
so warm inside them.

THE SEA, THE SEA

Now that they are not
lovers, love is

a great power again.

Like shells later found
on a mountaintop,
someone asks what receded

for these to be here?

A great power,
and there is not an only

life this happens to.

AUBADE

Love is so early in us,

so early and therefore
no wonder it is a child,

in the hand-firstness
of darkness

it is a child, it is a child

of such honey
and the rages made.

Not every part of us
can be a child, anymore.

Stay small, little one,
while you can.

FOR THE DARK AND BLAZING TRUTHS

And, we had not made the world.

First we were forced,
then freed to believe

we belong here. We are certain

of nothing except we are
not dead, and the dead are

more than us
and harder to love.

And we had not made the world—

or the water raising a family of waters,
or the wind retenanting the trees,
or the squirrels that mete out their meals
in tiny minefields, or the father and the mother

who will end, on an Earth
that will end,

a detention desired
in the school
of our no longer being
children.

ADDENDUM

Who was it said: "AND

is the greatest
      miracle"? Praise

be his/her name.

ALL THOSE THAT WANDER

After the ark survived the Flood,
it was taken apart
to be made into cages.

This is the nature of religion.

BESTIARY

I want to tell you I have grown

and become acquainted
with the cages
and am myself, admittedly,

a cage, only it is
      a cage that will let

the creature out.

PRETERNATURAL

We didn't know there were coyotes
till the disappearance
of the little dogs, or deer until
the windshields shattered.

Brazen as death among the daylights,
a returning to us
of the said-goodbye-to
garden. "Armageddon," cried some;

others, "The end
of the End
of Among."

ELEGY

Above all, beneath all,

in as many ways
      as the spider has

known the wall,

     I miss and am
member of you
and of that race the grass
grows thru.

AN ITHACA

In the Odyssey,
the bed is made of a rooted and immovable tree,
a living tree, and all about the sleeping
body are birds.

I had thought we would arrive at a total dwelling-place,

where other than human voices
could wake us, a solidarity
across the creatures, in a field

where once was
so a war.

PART TWO

BIG TREE ROOM

It is hard to keep remaining whole

as for the leviathan to stay
surfaced is hard. The United

States "are" (said Whitman) not "is"

a unativity,
fragile, concomitant,

the "e" in men for
       ever mending

from an "a"

. . .

is hard, and therefore a task, to perpetuate

the gesture of welcome,
        to be *native* only ever

meant born and we are

old. We have not been
born for a while.

. . .

It is hard and, therefore, a task to keep remaining

here, a kind of continuous
creature like a lawn
which is grass after grass
and hard and there

fore a task to perpetuate the stasis: "I am

blue," says the breeze
thru the sky. "I am law," say the trees

of their felled
selves, the pages.

. . .

We are here. Together. Under the public

and touchable trees. Blue sky
in town today and too I think to add you

are not, or I, a wall. We are with all
whose walls have fallen and are there

fore visitable. We are here
and would mind
what happens here. And it is a good

day, the one
        that finds us

naked.

US

where others with their wax and feathers failed.
GEORGE OPPEN

I say "bird" and watch
as the word

makes its way to you. (Faith in this, tho all

the field's
    a semaphore

meaning *never to let it*

land.)

LITTLE HOUSE

Do you really think we failed?

I think who we are is not finally
how we live
with one person.

It's how we behave
in the Field.

ON RE-READING WALDEN

Who has not loved
who could

teach them?

It is one thing to exist in uncertainty
but to exist among another's,

without
sympathy

entirely obscuring the view, over
and above belonging,

who has not loved who could

head them beyond
the merely habitable?

Among things that have failed

to be free, or are
            still preparing

to be, find me.

TO EARTHWARD

For its being

not one
thing was why

I came. Only

to be told I must find the one
person, the one
purpose. Concessions

to finitude,
            concessions

to finitude!

As from each cell—
some kept or as yet
unkept or still to be
kept promise continues
this its towarding.

A LEXICON

WORD

To be placed in the middle of the mouth,
where no consonants come.

WORD

To speak on all-fours in the forest
down the dark, deciduous halls.

WORD

To tell the battle its war is over,
to be carved in stones and, also, coming.

WORD to be cried out
from the base of all
ladders, to be legible
across the creatures.

TROUBADOUR

Someone enters: That alone
makes me speak.

When you lived, I spoke to you.
We are transitive.

I never dream of speech:
I either speak or don't.

And now that I know
where you will not be—

I do not go there.

TILL HUMAN VOICES WAKE US

In the history of language,
       the first obscenity was silence.

MEGAPHONE

(The future

isn't what will be
come of us
but with whom we

will speak.)

FOR FAR

There is a Zulu phrase for *far*
which means where a man cries,

"Mother, I am lost."

            If there is one for *near*
      I do not know it.

It may be where a man does not need
to cry. Or cries,

"Leave me, mother."

BELL

Come here, what

son, what
daughter, what

may. *Come here*

were the first furthest words,
the elsewhereing tracks

of our animal.

Thru bird corridors of yellow
pine or chestnut,
treated with creosote, come.

There is
only the one
call ever.

MANIFEST

When we had reached the West

the sun delivered
its last instruction. *Nearness,*

it said, *nearness*
is the new frontier.

FIXED STARS GOVERN

We are rescued, yes.

We are brought back
into patterns we are put,

no longer at the noon
of our adventure.

A light is on, only it is
our light we are

rescued by. We are
brought back
into houses we are put.

There is a light in each
window, only it is

a lamp to read our battles by.

The hero is the one
who moves
forward in the dark,
as Seferis said.

DISSENT

In the kingdom
      of images, the blink

is the infidel—

PEACEABLE

Of what is this

gesture

the ancestor?

The question, and not the answer, is
the only Bible in our house.

FUNDAMENT

I was not the only one who felt these things.
JACK SPICER

One of us died
on the stairs, which began

with the Mayans

using root and rock
for foothold.

Another died at our desk,
which was a tree
or two, or on the phone,

which was a far-cry.

And one or two or three of us were on fire, though one cannot be
or two or three on fire long, or one or more is not long in falling,
falling is what it is called but not by those that fall who are all too beyond
and involved to call it. And tens or more of us died of the building itself.

Road, why is there
road here?

In the room, in the inner
air, why is there
there *here?* All the living

are too young to know.

TRANSCRIPT

There was some

thing not
visible that was

a scar. "It had been

a normal morning." "We had lived
a normal life." "He wasn't supposed
to be there...." Not to have been there
was what all were supposed to be.

In the presence
of the unfinished we are

invited to look
in both directions, in case

the Empty is us.

UNKNOWN, THE

And so I will not learn you *language*, you *man on the corner*
of Fourth and Ninth, will not know you
nations, will not read you *Bible, atomic chart,*
not eat you off your birthplace *berries*, will not start any
more to finish you *thesis, tome*, not find you

grail-man, not find you
grail-woman, not get over

you grail-
stone, grail,
stone.

SPHINX HOUR

I said to the man, "I do not know

if I am a good
or a bad." He said, "To be a good person

you must first be a great animal."

And so I let the crawl
come unto me.

EVENSONG

Little bird, what is your friend?

The wind, said the finch.

And your enemy, tell me his name,
so I may point him
with every of my arrows? *The wind*,

said the finch, *and all
its wind-folk.*

FLOCK

But she was glad to be looking

and them not
       always to arrive

was like

love is
love of

a future.

O CLOCK

There have been things I,
instead of time,
have all by myself destroyed.

I, instead of
    time, anticipating

the Time.

THE LONG NOW

And in the center of the courtyard, a tree,

under which we
spread ourselves,

nearness closing the eyes
as, in faith,
the farness does.

For a moment, our limbs were in the continuous
touch of the crawl we came from, the third wall
was fourthed. Time within us, without us.

There is a saying that towards the forest
came an axeman and one tree said

to the others, *Fear not,*

for the handle
is one of us.

Love the destroyer,
love the preserver,
wherever you are now
is one of us.

CONCORD

I have measured the distance

(from here to there)

            (from me to you)

(from birth to death)

and it is not far. We could be there
this evening with our bared feet

and our first names.

What at birth was proposed to us,
what at walking was perceived
over the man-high grasses, what keeps

never coming,

       let steps be

found again.

AN ETHIC

Or, as Thoreau replied
      to the deathbed question,

"What do you see?"

One
world at a
time.

NOTES

FURTHERMORE: "One has to believe furthermore in the voyage of others" is a line from Jorie Graham's *Sea Change*. The poem is dedicated to my mother, who brought us through.

ALL THOSE THAT WANDER: After J.R.R. Tolkien's "not all those that wander are lost."

FOR THE DARK AND BLAZING TRUTHS: The title is an adaptation of a line from George Oppen's "Neighbors," and the incanted phrase is taken from a poem by Kenneth Patchen.

BIG TREE ROOM: After the "Big Tree Room" in Yosemite National Park.

TILL HUMAN VOICES WAKE US: The title echoes a line by George Oppen ("human voices wake us, or we drown"), which in turn echoes a line by T.S. Eliot ("human voices wake us, and we drown").

FOR FAR: The Zulu etymology is derived from Martin Buber's *I-Thou*.

BELL: The opening line is a play on the first phrase spoken over the telephone: "Mr. Watson—come here." The poem is dedicated to Alexander Graham Bell, who passed away on August 2, 1922 (the same date I was born a half-century later) and to my father who devoted his life to Bell Laboratories and to the possibilities of telephony (literally, far speech).

FIXED STARS GOVERN: "Fixed stars govern a life" is a line by Sylvia Plath. The final lines allude to a poem by George Seferis.

TRANSCRIPT: The quotes were drawn from the 9/11 Oral History Project, based at Columbia University.

THE LONG NOW: The title honors "The Long Now" project, which sought to support long-term ecological and cultural thinking and used as one of its central analogies the trees at New College, Oxford University. Dedicated to my dear friend & ethicist David Rodin.

ISBN: 978-1-937658-09-0

Typesetting by HR Hegnauer
Text set in Garamond and Abadi

Cover photograph courtesy of the National Park Service,
Sequoia & Kings Canyon National Parks.

Cataloging-in-publication data is available
From the Library of Congress

Distributed by University Press of New England
One Court Street
Lebanon, NH 03766
www.upne.com

Nightboat Books
Callicoon, New York
www.nightboat.org

NIGHTBOAT BOOKS

Nightboat Books, a nonprofit organization, seeks to develop audiences for writers whose work resists convention and transcends boundaries. We publish books rich with poignancy, intelligence, and risk. Please visit our website, www.nightboat.org, to learn about our titles and how you can support our future publications.

This book was made possible by a grant from The Fund for Poetry.

The following individuals have supported the publication of this book. We thank them for their generosity and commitment to the mission of Nightboat Books:

Kazim Al i
Elizabeth Motika
Benjamin Taylor

This book has been made possible, in part, by a grant from the New York State Council on the Arts Literature Program.

CHRISTINA DAVIS is the author of *Forth A Raven* (Alice James Books, 2006). A graduate of the University of Pennsylvania and Oxford University, she is the recipient of the Witter Bynner Award from the Library of Congress, selected by U.S. poet laureate Kay Ryan, and residencies at the MacDowell Colony, Yaddo, and the James Merrill House. She currently serves as curator of the Woodberry Poetry Room, Harvard University, and lives in Cambridge, Massachusetts.